Smokey Finds His Spark!

by
Ann Melim

Illustrated by
Ben McGuire

Copyright © 2024 Ann Melim
Third Edition 2024 Ann Melim
All rights reserved.
Paperback ISBN: 978-1-915911-41-4
Hardback ISBN: 978-1-962973-99-1

Cover and Interior Design by Ben McGuire

Printed in the United States of America.

No part of this publication shall be reproduced, transmitted, or sold in whole or in part in any form without prior written consent of the author, except as provided by the United States of America copyright law. Any unauthorized usage of the text without express written permission of the publisher is a violation of the author's copyright and is illegal and punishable by law. All trademarks and registered trademarks appearing in this guide are the property of their respective owners.

For permission requests, write to the publisher,
addressed "Attention: Permissions Coordinator," at the address below.
abmelim01@gmail.com

Ordering Information: Quantity sales and special discounts are available on quantity purchases by corporations, associations, and others. For details, contact the publisher at abmelim01@gmail.com The information contained within this book is strictly for informational purposes. The material may include information, products, or services by third parties. As such, the Author and Publisher do not assume responsibility or liability for any third-party material or opinions.

Please visit www.SmokeyFindsHisSpark.com for more information about the Smokey Series.

This book is dedicated to my brother,
Seth.

A lover of animals, whichever he finds.
Cows and birds and dogs of all kinds.
Stay true to your colors and I think you will see,
That all creatures will love you, especially me.

Based on a true story.

Carrier pigeon 603497 was trained under a smoggy sky
Every morning, noon and night,

By Bigwig, the Sergeant,
To carry messages by flight.

Pigeon 603497 was kept in a small cage in the dark,
Where he was **sad** and **lonely**, which dimmed his spark.

He **glowed** on the inside but no one could see,
How special he was and what he could be.

He had so much potential.
Perhaps in the end,
He could wear his **spark** proudly
With the help of a friend.

And then came the honor,
Time for him to fly,
To carry his message
Through wide open sky.

Checking the tag before the bird flew off,
Bigwig barked sternly with a shout like a cough,

"If you should stop, don't ever come back!!!
For you will be useless; determination you lack."

And so the nameless bird
Took off and then flew
For thousands of miles,
So **tired** he grew.

From the wind and the rain, the snow and the sleet,
The small carrier pigeon grew sad in **defeat.**

Thirsty and hungry. Ashamed and scared.
The young bird then landed, not moving, just stared.

Then along came Miss Mallory,
A young girl of ten

Who said,

**I'll love you.
I'll feed you.
I'll do what I can.**

She cut off his tag, nameless no longer.
"I'll call you **Sir Smokey** and you will grow stronger."

"I'll make a soft bed with straw and some hay,
Where you will be safe and grow bigger each day."

Miss Bellie, Miss Weenie, Miss Rosie, Miss Jenn.

The hens are real friendly,
Unkind they are not.
You'll see you're so lucky
With the home you have got.

Miss Rosie, the Big Bird, took him under her wing
And said to him softly, "tonight I will sing

**For all of my babies, both old and the new
So you can dream sweetly the entire night through.**

There is no more Bigwig, darkness or cages.
You are now **free** to live here ages and ages.

Miss Mallory covered them with quilts and tucked them in tight, And whispered to all, "I love you, goodnight."

**Smokey glowed from the inside and was happy to be
Seen for how special he was and now we shall see
The SPARK in young Smokey begin to shine through.
With the help of your friends, you can shine too.**

Questions for the reader

How did Bigwig make you feel?

If Smokey's spark makes him special, what is your spark? What makes you special?

How many ♡ can you find in the book?

Which hen do you like most? Why?

What do you think will happen next for Smokey? Will he go on more adventures?

Smokey's Story

One day my younger brother Seth found a homing pigeon in distress on a walkway at his work. The poor pigeon was obviously exhausted and in desperate need of help. He wore tags on his ankles, signifying that he never made it to a specific destination.

After some research, Seth was able to contact the bird's owner. The owner's reply was to simply leave the bird alone; that he was useless now that he had not been able to make his journey.

Seth took the bird home to his daughter Mallory. She named him Smokey and he lived with their hens while he recovered. Who knows what adventures are in Smokey's future?

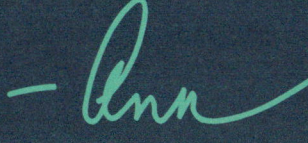

A portion of the proceeds from this book will go

Wings of the Dawn

Wildlife Rehabilitation Center and Bird Sanctuary

Wings of the Dawn strives to provide the best wildlife rehabilitation services possible. With every rescue, their goal is to rehabilitate the animal back to full health and release it back into the wild. They believe that each animal should live in as natural a habitat as possible.

Wings of the Dawn provides professional and humane care in all phases of wildlife rehabilitation, respecting the wildness and maintaining the dignity of each animal in life and in death.

They strive to rehabilitate and release each animal back to the wild in a healthy state that will insure their survival.

For more information, please go to
www.wingswildlife.org

About the Author

Ann Melim is a New Hampshire native and retired high school English teacher of twenty- two years. After retiring, Ann delved into writing memoir essays and is in the process of compiling these into a book. When she is not writing, one can find her walking her favorite dogs around town, hiking, kayaking and driving her Model A Ford. Ann is the proud mother of Isabel, her daughter who attends Assumption University and wife to Joseph, her husband of twenty three years. With the support of her husband, Ann has been able to reach this milestone of publishing her first book.

She continues to teach and facilitate discussions through her memoir book club and is driven by stories of adversity, determination and perseverance, much like the story within these pages.

About the Illustrator

Somewhere around age six, Ben McGuire started telling everyone that he had decided to become an artist. Some people told him that he couldn't make a living as an artist. They were right. (Just kidding) He's been a professional artist his entire life and is doing just fine. So, don't listen to people who say you can't do it. Work hard. You got this.

Ben lives with his dog Frank... oh, and also with his son Connor, his daughter Amber, and his wife Shannon. There are also two cats who run the house he lives in. It's probably time for them to eat again.

Ben loves snowboarding, pickleball, skateboarding, science fiction and fantasy role playing games, and absolutely kills it at karaoke.

Glossary

Carrier Pigeon — In history, carrier pigeons were used to carry messages long distances. Now, many people raise them and send them on long distance journeys as a hobby.

Spark — Something that makes you special and one of a kind.

Smoggy — Dirty fog

Dimmed — To make less bright.

Defeat — To lose.

Determination — To continue through difficult conditions.

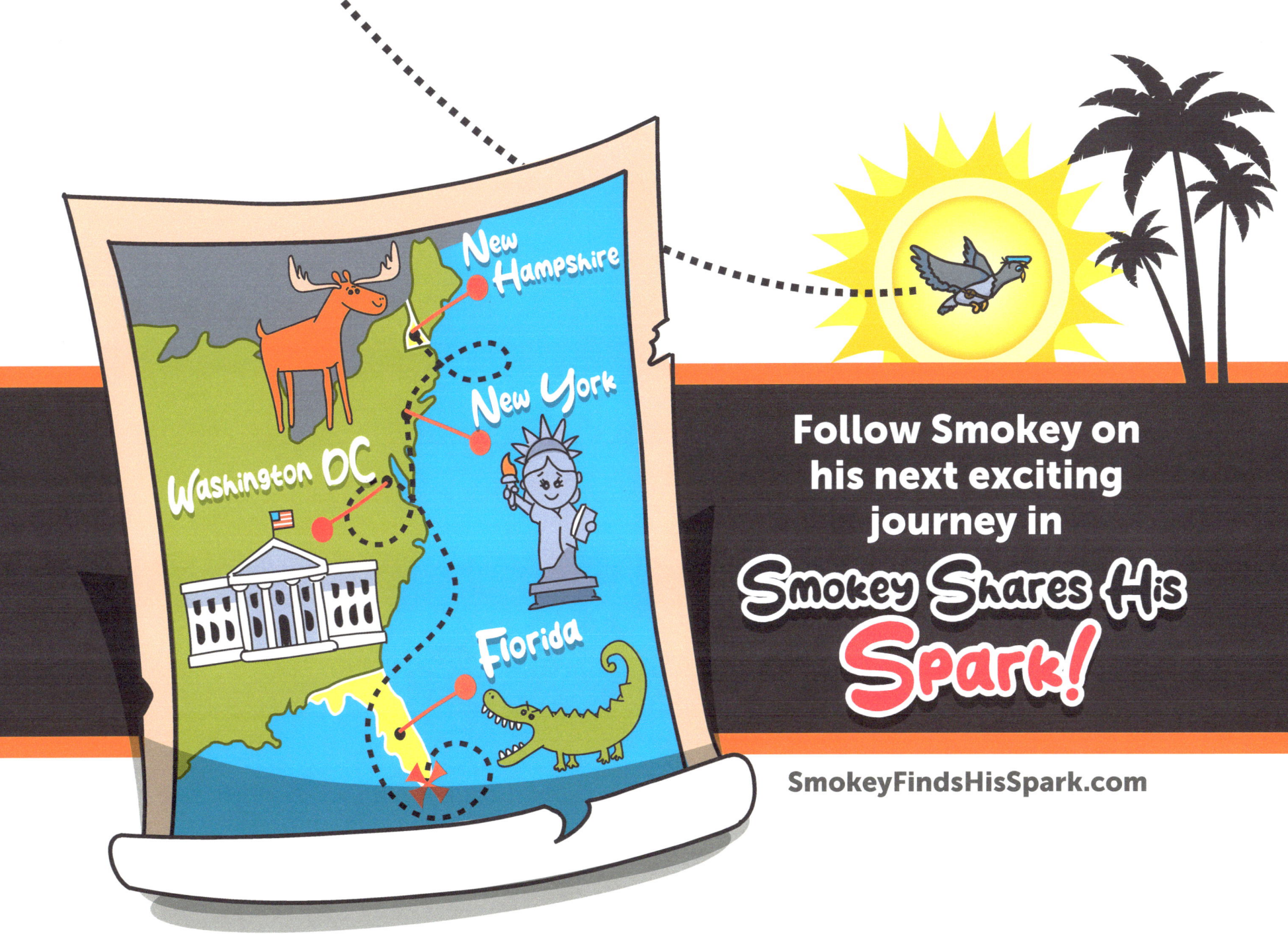

www.ingramcontent.com/pod-product-compliance
Lightning Source LLC
Chambersburg PA
CBHW042106090526

44590CB00004B/117